ISBN: 978-1-912484-32-8
Published by Angelis Publications
www.angelispublications.com

Welcome to the Celebration of

On:

At:

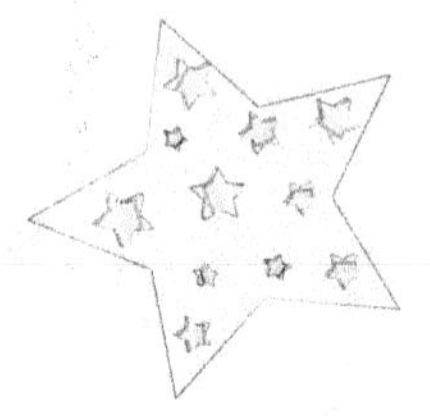

Have a Great Time!

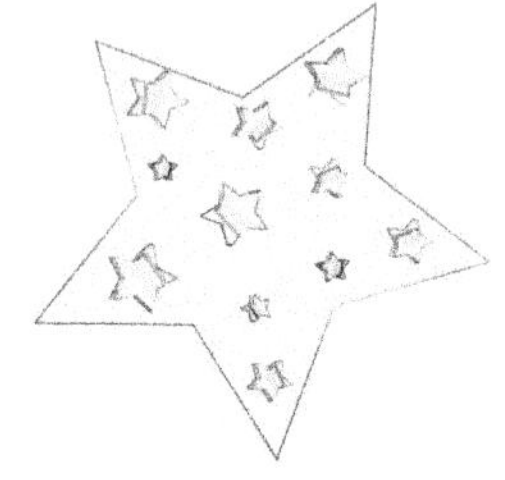

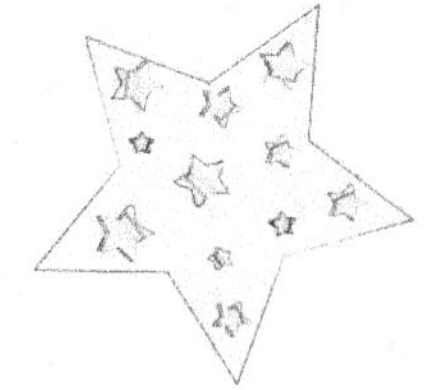

Name

Messages

Name

Messages

Name	Messages

Name

Messages

Name

Messages

Name

Messages

Name

Messages

Name

Messages

Name

Messages

Name

Messages

Name

Messages

Name

Messages

Name

Messages

Name

Messages

Name

Messages

Name

Messages

Name

Messages

Name

Messages

Name

Messages

Name

Messages

Name

Messages

Name

Messages

Name

Messages

Name

Messages

Name

Messages

Name

Messages

Name

Messages

Name

Messages

Name

Messages

Name

Messages

Name

Messages

Name

Messages

Name

Messages

Name

Messages

Name

Messages

Name

Messages

Name

Messages

Name

Messages

Name

Messages

Name

Messages

Name

Messages

Name

Messages

Name

Messages

Name

Messages

Name

Messages

Name

Messages

Name

Messages

Name Messages

Name

Messages

Name

Messages

Name

Messages

Name

Messages

Name

Messages

Name

Messages

Name

Messages

Name

Messages

Name

Messages

Name

Messages

Name

Messages

Name

Messages

Name

Messages

Name

Messages

Name

Messages

Name

Messages

Name

Messages

Name

Messages

Name

Messages

Name

Messages

Name

Messages

Name	Messages

Name

Messages

Name

Messages

Name

Messages

Name

Messages

Name

Messages

Name

Messages

Name

Messages

Name

Messages

Name

Messages

Name

Messages

Name

Messages

Name

Messages

Name

Messages

Name

Messages

Name

Messages

Name

Messages

Name

Messages

Name

Messages

Name

Messages

Name

Messages

Name

Messages

Name

Messages

Name

Messages

Name

Messages

Name

Messages

www.ingramcontent.com/pod-product-compliance
Lightning Source LLC
Chambersburg PA
CBHW080809020826
48982CB00016B/858

* 9 7 8 1 9 1 2 4 8 4 3 4 8 *